# The Joy of Connection

# How to Find Your Coaching Niche

With all my love

ENRICO MASSANI

*Per te, Mamma.*

*Tu nous as appris à marcher. Tu nous as appris à parler. Tu as mis un toit au dessus de nos têtes, et tu nous as toujours nourri. Tu nous as appris les choses importantes de la vie. Tu nous as guidé dans les moments difficiles.*

*Quand nous étions enfants, tu étais toujours là pour nous consoler, pour nous cajoler. Ta chaleur et ta voix nous redonnait de la vigueur et nos soucis s'evanouissaient.*

*Pour tout ce que tu nous as appris, l'amour que tu nous as donné, nous te remercions.*

*Maman, merveilleux ton sourire, ta vivacité, ta joie de vivre nous manquerons à jamais.*

# CONTENTS

ENRICO MASSANI

## ACKNOWLEDGMENTS

A sincere thank-you to my partner, George, for his patience and support, and for giving me the space to write this book. To my Dad and my brother, Paolo, a heartfelt thank-you, as I wasn't always there for you when I needed space. To my mentors who inspired and guided me through the years of distilling and honing my message. Last, but not least, to the clients, messengers, coaches, consultants, healers and light workers who gave generously of their time, feedback and encouragement to allow this message to come forth.

*"Joy can only be real if people look upon their life as a service and have a definite object in life outside themselves and their personal happiness."*

*Leo Tolstoy*

ENRICO MASSANI

# INTRODUCTION

For many years I have operated two parallel careers, as an Internet Marketer and as a Business Coach.

My curiosity to learn all I could about how to optimize business success has driven me to amass an encyclopaedic knowledge of what is working online and to establish a thriving SEO Marketing Consultancy.

My passion for coaching and, in particular, for mentoring coaches, allows me the privilege of guiding the messengers to deliver their message.

My dual role as a coach and a marketer has also afforded me a unique insight into why some coaches thrive and others struggle to survive.

I was in the ideal position to observe how coaches presented their message to prospective clients and to analyse the techniques they employed.

The more I worked with coaches marketing their business, the more a startling pattern began to emerge.

I found that I could show coaches exactly the same methods; how to build a state-of-the-art, Google-optimised website and design powerful social media campaigns. However, even when all of these coaches applied the same marketing strategies and did all the right things in the right sequence, their results fell into two very different categories.

One group of coaches was attracting a steady flow of their ideal clients – people they loved to work with and who enjoyed working with them – while the other group, applying the same tried and tested marketing techniques, was struggling to see any response to their marketing efforts.

What I discovered was that the coaches who thrived were the coaches who were clear on their niche and their message.

What's more, you could see that their message resonated with them. They were in alignment with their purpose and loving their work. They were operating from a state of *joy*.

On the other hand, the coaches who were failing to attract or keep clients, were out of sync with their true purpose and were attempting to deliver a message that was not resonating with their authentic self. As a result, their message was vague or unclear, or even in conflict with their core values.

**The disconnect with clients was simply a reflection of their *own* disconnect with their message.**

These coaches were operating from a state of *struggle*.

The struggling coach comes to me in pain, at a loss to understand why they are trying so hard and achieving so little. They are confused, frustrated and exhausted, and usually running out of money! They have invested so much in training programmes and marketing and are still not seeing any return on their investment. They don't know what to try next – and time is running out!

If that sounds like you, I'm so happy you are here. You are here because you know it is time to surrender the struggle and to discover the joy of connection.

For, whatever you have tried before, or whatever doesn't seem to be working – whether you believe it to be a difficult market, competition, toxic clients, Google algorithms or a Facebook ban – it all boils down to the same cause:

**If you are not clear on who you are, the message you deliver and the exact niche you serve, you will continue to struggle.**

The good news is that all that *can* be fixed – and fixed quite quickly! I often see coaches get clarity in their niche after only one or two sessions.

That clarity can flip the switch from struggle to joy, literally overnight!

The sad news is that few coaching programmes are teaching 'How to Find Your Niche'. They may even be dispensing misleading advice, such as 'it's OK to just date a niche'. Some may advise you to 'listen to your heart' – but what if you don't know how to do that?

If you are called to coaching, you are called because you have a unique message to deliver, and there is a specific group of people waiting for that message. Until you get clear on that message, that group of people will continue to suffer without the solution you offer.

I wrote this book for you. It is my heart's desire that you discover that your niche is **not** 'out there somewhere'. It cannot be figured out or copied second-hand from what's working for someone else.

It is **who you are.**

You heart already knows your unique purpose.

So why can't you see it yet?

It's time to find out.

Are you ready to move from struggle to joy?


*Enrico Massani,*

*Edinburgh,*
*May 2017*


*If you have any questions or comments, or would like further information, I would be delighted to hear from you. Contact me at:*

*hello@thejoyofconnection.com*

*Enrico*

*"Find a place inside where there is joy and the joy will burn out the pain."*

*Joseph Campbell*

# CHAPTER 1

## IT ALL BEGINS FROM KNOWING WHO YOU ARE

*"Know thyself."* Socrates

**Before you can connect with your clients, you must first connect with yourself.**

It is often stated that the principles of coaching are universal and may be applied to help anyone to achieve anything.

Unfortunately, many coaches misinterpret this to mean that their core values and unique purpose are irrelevant, and that they should just pick a niche, get started, and work out the details as they go along.

However, your potential to do **anything** must never be used as an excuse to avoid taking the time to identify and define that **one thing** that reflects your authentic self and your highest value in serving others.

Failure to get absolutely clear on your **something** – the essence of exactly who you are and what you offer – is neglecting to establish the very foundation of your business, on which all other marketing efforts will stand or fall.

As you seek to promote what you do, any small discrepancy between **who you are** and **what you say** will become apparent, leading to conflicting signals which are insufficiently powerful to resonate with the audience you wish to engage.

You will either find yourself working with clients who are not a good fit for you or spending more time *coaxing* than coaching.

The importance of spending the time and ***doing the work to get clarity*** from the outset cannot be over-emphasised.

*"Clarity is power – the clearer you are about EXACTLY what it is you want, the more your brain knows how to get there."* Author Unknown

Every hour spent distilling your essence and honing your message *before* you start marketing will reap dividends. This time is never wasted – it has the potential to save months, or even years, of confusion and frustration further down the line, as you seek to understand why clients are not responding to a vague or contradictory statement of intent.

I work with coaches to get clear on who they are and to find their message. Clients come to me in pain, after months or years of struggle and trying to understand why they are struggling to connect with the clients they feel drawn to serve.

Coaches know that they have a calling. However, that strong sense of vocation and the desire to get started often means that they have attempted to implement the 'How' to run a coaching business before they are sure of the 'What' – the message they are called to deliver.

If you have spent a lot of time and money on training, it may seem logical to just get started and work it all out as you go along.

If that sounds like you, ask yourself "How's that working for you?"

Getting started before getting clear on your message is what I call '**Upside-Down Marketing**'.

If you have been told that it's OK to just date your niche, and get started, with the assurance that you can always get clear or switch niches later, then I'm afraid you have fallen victim to some bad advice.

Not only are you setting yourself up for the pain of disconnection from your true purpose, you are failing to harness the power of the Search Engines to connect you with your ideal clients.

In fact, it's even more serious than that. If you have started to build a coaching practice in one niche, then switched niches, or re-branded your message a few times, you have already begun to prime the Search Engines to divide and dilute your online identity.

Google works by knowing **who you are** from the start. Everything you do online contributes to your unique digital footprint.

If your message and your website keep changing, you are sending out inconsistent, or even contradictory, signals each time you swap niches, re-brand, try out different strategies or repackage your website.

Not only will you struggle to know who you are, but Google will struggle to identify you.

That's right: the Search Engines require a clear, strong signal and they will work for you when you get clear on who you are.

If the Search Engines can't identify you, how will your ideal clients connect with you?

Don't panic – it's not irreversible, yet – but I do urge you to get clear now, rather than continue to move forward with a vague or inauthentic message.

Any disconnect between you and your authentic message will be reflected in disconnect between you and your clients.

If left unchecked, this disconnect will not diminish or resolve itself through time, but will continue to lead you away from your real purpose, resulting in more doubt, more effort and more struggle.

In other words, you will move further out of Joy.

Joy is your natural state and it comes from knowing exactly who you are and what you stand for.

If your coaching business is not connected to your Joy, it's time to examine how you got here.

*"Live in Harmony with your highest values and your innermost convictions. Never compromise."*

*Brian Tracy*

# CHAPTER 2

## FIVE WARNING SIGNS THAT YOU ARE NOT IN THE RIGHT NICHE

If your coaching practice is not attracting the clients who resonate with your message and who understand your value, you are not clear on your coaching niche.

**Notice:** that does not mean that you are a bad coach or that you should be seeking out another career. It means exactly what it says:

 **You have not taken the time to get clear on who you are, what you do, and exactly how you deliver that to the people you serve.**

Now that might not be your fault, because so many programmes are teaching that it's not necessary to get clear on a niche. They might even encourage you to just try out a few ideas, and see how it goes.

As I said before, that is bad advice and it does not serve you.

If you have received this misleading advice, and have just picked a niche without really getting to the core of who you are and what message you deliver, then your coaching practice will be hard to market, and you may recognize some, or all, of the following warning signs.

### WARNING SIGN 1:  Good Training Programmes Work for Other People, but Not for You

Your fellow students on a coaching course achieve massive breakthroughs and success. You are happy to see them succeed and grateful for the evidence that it *can* be done, but mystified by *your* inability to make it work, with your inner voice pleading, "Why not me?"

So why *do* some coaches seem to be able to implement the training and get great results, while you follow the same instructions diligently, yet still fail to attract clients?

Is there something wrong with you?

You'll be pleased to learn that there is nothing wrong with you, and failure to get results from the training courses does not mean you are any less competent – or that you should just give up coaching and go do something else!

If you are reading this book, I am fairly certain that you are a coach – albeit a coach who is not yet running their ideal business in the way they would like.

To understand why you must get clear on your niche, you must remember that coaching is not just another job, and you can't build a coaching practice by applying old 'job search' strategies. It's not enough to just copy what is working for other people. Other people are **not You**.

Coaching is not a career, it's a calling. Your calling is rooted in who you are, and it cannot be calculated from external factors. Coaching is meeting people heart-to-heart. We describe ourselves as heart-centred coaches, and yet we have locked our heart out of the most important step!

You see, the training programmes and marketing strategies are sound, but they show you the logistics of **How** to set up and market a coaching business, not the 'exactly **What** is your niche' information necessary to make it work!

The programmes and marketing techniques **will** work for you – **once you are clear on your message.**

Unfortunately, many of the training programmes either skip through the 'Finding your Niche' section, as if it's not that important, or tell you that it's alright to just pick any niche for now and work it out as you go along!

This is probably the worst advice a heart-centred coach could receive.

Some of the courses actually **do** teach that you must 'listen to your heart' in order to get clear on your niche – but they leave it up to you to figure out exactly how to do that!

The coaches who make the training work are the ones who are **clear** on their niche.

The coaches who can't make the system work are not any less technical, lucky or capable, they are simply not clear on their niche.

Resolve that one issue, and you will find that the courses and the marketing techniques will begin working for you.

## **WARNING SIGN 2 : Shiny Object Syndrome**

If you have been struggling to figure out why the coaching training courses are not working for you, and blaming it on some piece of the method that is missing, then chances are that you are constantly on the look-out for the latest online marketing techniques and tricks.

You flit from one course to the next, investing in more and more training, convinced that the next one will be the answer to the problem. However, even with great intentions, enthusiasm and substantial investment of time and money, you find you are no further forward and still struggling to attract clients.

For many coaches, this is an all-too-familiar pattern. Their desire to serve others is strong and they believe they are being blocked because they can't find that elusive missing link in their marketing strategy.

Often they come to me as a last resort, when they have tried everything else and are at their wit's end trying to understand why they can't get their message across.

It is my sincere wish that this book will reveal the real reason why you are stuck – and why no amount of training or advertising will repair a vague or inconsistent message that does not come from your heart.

In truth, there is nothing to find. You are not lacking a message or a purpose. You just haven't been shown how to interpret the message your heart has been transmitting all along!

More often than not, that's not the fault of the experienced coach who has taught you, for many of the coaching mentors and trainers fail to understand this phenomenon.

Like natural talents, some niches are more obvious than others. If you are a world-class sportsman or a musical genius, your talent is fairly obvious, and it doesn't take much effort to work out what you should be doing.

However, for many of us, our unique gift is less apparent, and usually takes more time to define.

That doesn't mean you should just give up and copy what someone else is doing, but that's exactly what many coaches are being encouraged to do!

## WARNING SIGN 3 : Toxic Clients

Do you have clients who don't show up on time, miss sessions, don't pay on time (or at all!) or who simply don't take action on the work they agreed with you? They are not convinced of your ability to help them or fail to see how the coaching is working –

constantly questioning your methods or making excuses for not implementing the changes required to get the results they want.

Or they may be enthusiastic about participating in free coaching, but less interested when asked to invest financially.

A tell-tale indicator of whether you are clear on your message, or not, is how clients and potential clients respond to you.

When you are clear on who you are, the unique message you bring and how you deliver that, your ideal clients will be drawn to you.

When you are working with your ideal clients, it will be a source of joy – these are the people you love to work with! They will resonate with what you offer, recognise the value of your message for them and happily pay for the results you bring them. You will not have to persuade, coax or force people into your coaching practice.

The main reason why coaches are suffering from exhaustion is that they are trying to spread the net too wide. They are trying to make the message as vague and as multi-purpose as possible, in the mistaken belief that this will expand their potential target market. In fact, it has the opposite, and often catastrophic, effect.

In the attempt to market to everyone, they are failing to reach the specific community they have come to serve.

## WARNING SIGN 4 : Confusion

You may have tried numerous methods and approaches to launch your coaching practice, but to little or no avail.

You have crafted websites, opt-in pages, and sales letters. You have written Facebook pages and Free Reports, and offered free coaching sessions.

When the strategy doesn't appear to be working with one niche, you try another niche. You change your logo, your marketing slogan. Still no breakthrough.

You may even go right back to the beginning and start from scratch, employing all the latest advice from your coaching mentors, and optimizing your marketing for Google. Still little response.

You reach the stage of despair – nothing works! There are so many things that could be wrong and you are overwhelmed, trying to patch up the perceived problems. You are confused about the next step to take and paralysed into inactivity.

There seem to be so many contributory factors that need to be resolved and so many half-finished coaching programmes that you have started and abandoned. You are at a loss to understand why it isn't working for you, and mentally drained by the sheer effort of trying.

You have reached stalemate and the very thought of marketing your coaching business is so overwhelming that you can't face it.

These are the all-too-familiar indicators that you are trying to promote a message that does not come from your authentic self.

You have been fooled into implementing Step 2 ('How' to run a coaching practice) before gathering the vital information for Step 1 ('What' is the unique solution you offer?).

If that is you, then you are actually **resisting** finding your niche.

Surprised?

You shouldn't be. For some people, their niche is obvious. For others it is hidden under years, decades of accumulated beliefs about who you are and your value.

 It takes **work** to peel back the layers of false beliefs and **courage** to trust that your genuine authentic self is much more valuable than any image your mind could construct for you.

If the thought of having to do the work to find your niche sounds daunting, ask yourself this:

"How much more daunting will it be to continue trying to promote a message that either doesn't resonate with Who I am, or that is so cryptic or vague that my potential clients can't find me?"

The really exciting news is that the work doesn't take long and I have seen people turn around their lives and coaching businesses after only a couple of session working with me.

Some take longer – it just depends on how much resistance they have built around finding who they really are and the unique, valuable message they have to contribute to the World. Once you get clear on that message, you can wave 'Goodbye' to the confusion for good.

When your confusion is replaced by **clarity**, your path becomes obvious, and you become connected to your source of true value. That connection will be mirrored in your connection to the clients who 'get' you and want to work with you.

When you know who you are and the solution you bring, and can clearly describe the community of people you have come to serve, you automatically gain the unwavering commitment of a mind in alignment with what your heart desires.

Your success becomes inevitable.

All that spadework you dug in building your coaching practice has not gone to waste – and you don't have to go back to the beginning to start all over again.

**So what are the two main excuses coaches use to avoid doing the work to get clear on their niche?**

<u>Excuse No.1</u>: **Coaching is a universal technique that can be applied to help anyone get from where they are now to where they want to be in the shortest time possible.**

Unfortunately, many coaches – and coaching consultants – interpret this to mean that a coach can build a coaching practice by coaching anything to anyone.

Well, theoretically, this is possible, but, in practice, this is no longer how the world of work operates.

Prior to the year 2000, you may have been conditioned to acquire a broad range of skills in order to appeal to as many employers as possible in a fixed geographical location.

You adopted the 'generalist' approach in order to 'get a job'.

However, I must emphasise that coaching is not just another job!

Coaching is a calling, and, since the arrival of the Internet, it has become imperative that you be able to define that calling, i.e. to become a 'specialist'.

It is vital that you do the work to drill down on exactly what sets you apart from the thousands or even millions offering similar coaching services, in order to  reach out and connect with your ideal clients online.

**Excuse. No.2**: **Many successful coaches have two or more niches**

You may have seen a coach build a practice in one niche, then diversify into another field, so that they have two or more parallel businesses.

It is important to note that they did not build those practices simultaneously. They first had to establish their presence and audience in one niche before setting up another.

The fact that some coaches happily run multiple coaching businesses in different fields is **not** evidence that identifying your specific niche is not important. The reason they became established at all was that they first got clear on their core niche and focused on building that, *before* leveraging their influence to launch another business.

## WARNING SIGN 5 : Doubt

This is the big one! **Doubt is an alarm signal from your heart.**

**It is a signal that cannot be suppressed, shut off or ignored. Any attempt to silence it in one area, will just see it re-appear in another – and screaming even louder to get your attention.**

Until you realise the importance of getting clear on your niche and your message, your progress will continue to be sabotaged by a heart that is not in alignment with what you are attempting to achieve.

You see, doubt is not a measure of uncertainty or a feeling that will fade once you gain confidence and get those clients.

Doubt is a direct signal from your heart that you are not connected to your unique purpose.

Your heart already knows your niche, your message, your purpose, your calling – whatever you want to call it – but, until you learn to listen to your heart, you will continue to look for the answers in the wrong place: your mind.

Your core values are stored in your heart. Although your heart already knows your life's purpose, somewhere along the road you have stopped listening to your heart when it comes to choosing your life's work.

You have been tricked into handing over this critical task to the mind.

Your poor mind! It has been over-worked trying to solve a puzzle without access to the necessary information.

In Douglas Adam's humorous work, "The Hitch-Hiker's Guide to the Galaxy", the supercomputer 'Deep Thought' was programmed to find the 'answer to the ultimate question of life, the universe and everything'. After 7.5 million years of calculations, it returned the answer '42'.

We laugh at the ludicrous disconnect between the question and the answer. However, coaches without clients are functioning from a similar state of disconnect. Your brain is a supercomputer with the power to bring you anything you programme it to do – but **only** when it is fed the necessary, correct information from the heart.

If you haven't programmed your mind with the information it needs from your heart, is it any wonder that your mind is exhausted, confused, frustrated, overwhelmed, frazzled and burnt-out from the strain?

Not only do you have a stressed, over-worked mind, your heart is crying out for your attention. Can you see the inconsistency of attempting to reach out to the hearts of others while you are disconnected from what your own heart is aching to tell you?

Can you see how your heart is pulling in the opposite direction from where your mind wants to go?

Trying to operate a coaching practice that does not have the support of your heart is like driving with the brakes on.

In the chapters that follow, I will address the reasons **why** and **how** heart-centred coaches are **resisting** getting clear on their niche.

*"Only the truth of who you are, if realized,*
*will set you free. "*

*Eckhart Tolle.*

# CHAPTER 3

# A  MESSAGE FROM YOUR HEART

For some people the concept of the heart is obvious.  For others, who have been taught to ignore the heart and to override the messages of the heart in favour of logical thought, the concept of the heart seems vague and esoteric. It's only a pump circulating blood around the body, right?

I use the word 'heart' to refer to the very core of who you are. It's the seat of your being, the essence of you that makes you unique and which drives everything you do.

If the concept of 'listening to your heart' seems strange or bewildering, and you are asking, "How do you do that?", let me remind me that you already know. You know how to trust your heart when it comes to relationships (matters of the heart) or the hobbies and pastimes that make your heart sing!

However, for many of us who grew up in the 20$^{th}$ Century and became so conditioned to 'get a job' rather than 'find our purpose', we were taught to disregard the heart when it came to work.

The limiting factor of geographical location often led us into a career that crushed our spirit, but that offered more opportunities for secure, paid employment than a career we would have loved to pursue.

For many, the approach of ignoring the heart in order to follow the money may have worked for a time, but then led to emotional breakdown later, when the strain of constantly working against the heart's purpose became too much – the classic midlife crisis!

Now that the Internet has freed us from the limitations of location, there is no excuse not to listen to what the heart is trying to tell us.

Notice the language you reach for when a situation or event impacts the very deepest, most authentic part of you.

Your dreams, aspirations and objectives are described as your **heart's desire**.

Sincere gratitude is delivered **from the heart**, and condolences expressed with **heart-felt** sympathy.

The burning need to achieve something means you have your **heart set on it**. When it doesn't happen you feel **disheartened**.

The end of a romantic relationship leaves you **heart-broken**.

Notice, also, how you express that feeling you get when you are trying to achieve something, but you would rather do almost anything instead. (*Hint:* that moment you realise you would rather re-paint the ceiling than write a post for your coaching blog!)

That intense resistance from the very depths of your being is **not** laziness or incompetence or a character flaw. It is what happens when **your heart's not in it**.

When your heart is not in it, you are not connected

to you. Your disconnection from your core will be reflected in how your ideal clients connect to you.

When your heart's not in it, you will have insufficient commitment to sustain the momentum necessary to connect with the people you have come to serve. Please note that commitment should not be confused with motivation, or *trying* harder or forcing yourself to overcome the resistance. Commitment is one of the effortless added benefits of working in alignment with your heart.

For, until your heart is in alignment with what your mind is attempting to achieve, your mind and your heart will continue to pull in opposing directions. There will always be resistance, overwhelm, doubt, confusion, frustration and brain fog –and it doesn't diminish through time. In fact, the further you progress, with a heart and brain which are not operating in parallel, the greater will be the divergence and the struggle.

Re-connecting with your heart and getting clear on who you are and the message you bring is not an optional step to be resolved *after* you establish your coaching practice.

Connecting with your heart is the **key** to connecting with your clients **now**.

# THE JOY OF CONNECTION

*"Don't let anyone tell you that you have to be a certain way. Be Unique. Be what you feel."*

*Melissa Etheridge*

# THE JOY OF CONNECTION

# CHAPTER 4

## YOUR UNIQUE PURPOSE

You are unique and you have a unique message to deliver – a particular solution to bring to a very specific group of people.

That group of people – I use the term 'your tribe', some say 'your peeps' – because it's easy to grasp the significance, even though I don't really like the terms – sometimes language is inadequate!

The general term is not important, but it is vital that you grasp the concept.

You are not randomly broadcasting an idea your mind constructed from your training, education, qualifications and past work experience.

The answer to finding your niche is not to be found in a formula that can be calculated from external factors, such as the demand for a particular service, or what seems to be working for other people.

You are not 'other people', you are **You**.

Any falsely constructed message that does not originate from who you are and the core values at the very heart of you, will be very difficult to relay to others.

If your message is not authentic, it will never truly resonate with you and any attempts to broadcast or share it with other people will be a constant uphill slog.

Unfortunately, many coaches are applying a strategy falsely-constructed from the mind's understanding of how sufficient interest will be generated to keep them solvent.

They may manage to implement that approach for a while, but it will feel like hard work.

**My message is to bring a message to the messengers.**

If you are reading this book, you are probably drawn to coaching and, as a coach, you have a vital and valuable message to deliver to a specific group of people who are waiting right now for you to step up to the plate and make contact with them.

However, the reason you are reading the book is because you are not effortlessly filling your coaching practice with hungry clients who are drawn to you and willing to pay you well for the solution you deliver.

I am so glad you are here, because it tells me that you are ready to fix that disconnect and finally find the missing piece of the puzzle.

The real reason your ideal clients are not showing up for you is because **you** are not showing up for them!

It could be that you are not congruent with your message or that your message does not adequately describe the solution you offer.

Either way, **You** are missing from your own message.

You see, it's not enough to figure out a niche or a service based on the **beliefs** your mind has about your value or your past experience or the demand for your services.

You cannot find your niche by deciding what is economically viable to the World in general, and expect to 'click' with enough random strangers to fill your coaching practice and 'earn a living'.

As I said before, your purpose cannot be worked out by your mind.

It is also misleading to think that you somehow have to 'find' your niche.

Your heart already knows your purpose, and has always known – there is nothing lost or missing.

However, the beliefs you acquired from the 20th Century strategy of 'getting a job' have handed over the task of 'finding your niche' to your mind, and, as I hope it is becoming clear to you, your mind does not have the information to do that.

The key to finding your niche is to do the work to get to know who you are and what you stand for.

This information lies in your heart – the core of you.

The real reason that you have failed to get clear on your niche is because the information of the heart is being obscured by layers of beliefs about work and your real value. It doesn't matter whether

45

those beliefs are 'true' or not, but they were formed by you in order to serve you in dealing with some life situation you have encountered at some time in the past.

It is necessary to discover which beliefs still serve you and which are simply obsolete programmes running in the background and which are obstructing the messages from your heart.

# THE JOY OF CONNECTION

*"Living up to an image that you have of yourself, or that other people have of you is inauthentic living."*

*Eckhart Tolle*

# THE JOY OF CONNECTION

# CHAPTER 5

## YOUR HIGHEST VALUE

If we accept that every person is unique and has a unique purpose to deliver to the World, we must also accept that each 'purpose' is equally valuable.

No one's message or gift or talent is more or less important than anyone else's.

However, we are children of the 20$^{th}$ Century!

Coaching is still quite a new concept for a lot of people, and most coaches setting up in business have come from a background in another field. In other words, you probably had a previous career, or at least one other job.

You grew up in the dying stages of what has been described as the 'Industrial Era' – a period in human history when it became easier to just find a job working for someone else, than to figure out your true vocation and work from your natural talents.

Not only did you grow up conditioned to get qualifications and get a job, but probably your parents and grandparents did too. By the time you were born, 'getting a job' had become the default and most 'secure' means of earning money.

Of course, now that full-time jobs are thin on the ground, it is neither the easiest nor the most secure option, but the belief persists that this is how human beings are designed to function.

Most of us have acquired false and limiting beliefs about money and our value to the World, formed because we, and the people who taught us (parents, teachers) grew up believing that our value to the World, and our financial success, depended on our ability to convince an employer to hire us.

Most of us experienced this. We chose a career

title based on the salary we could expect, the demand for our skills etc. We also expected to be judged by our job title. So we assumed false beliefs about job titles, such as doctor = impressive, hairdresser = not so much.

### Is a prestigious job title from a previous career blocking your view of who you really are?

As I said previously, your highest value **cannot** be figured out in your mind, and yet many coaches are allowing false beliefs about job titles to determine how they select or describe their niche.

They attempt to deduce their niche from a combination of their past experience, qualifications and what they *think* will impress other people – clients or friends and family.

They have learned to associate success and prestige with words such as 'manager', ' business owner', 'entrepreneur' and 'executive'. Of course, these words may actually appear in niche descriptions, but what do they actually describe and can we be certain that the community we wish to serve would recognize themselves in these descriptors?

These are simply examples – albeit some of the most common examples – of how coaches are failing to accurately describe the members of the tribe they serve.

To avoid the trap of using vague job titles which appear to be of value in the commercial world, it's vital to re-examine the true definition of 'value', and not to lose sight of the fact that everyone's purpose is equally valuable and, therefore, equally monetisable.

In contrast to your work currency in the Industrial Era, your value cannot be measured in terms of the value of your time to an employer.

Your **highest value** lies in what sets you apart; in what makes you **unique**.

It is **who you are**.

You can no more change that than change the colour of your eyes.

However, one of the biggest blocks that is facing our generation of coaches is the **fear** that:

**'The Real You will not be Good Enough'**

We have been so conditioned to design a 'best version' of ourselves, based on the beliefs we adopted from the Industrial Era strategy because:

Getting the Best Jobs depends on **Getting Ahead of the Competition.**

It is worth reminding ourselves of two important points here:

1. **Coaching is NOT a Job,** it is a Calling
2. When you function from what makes you unique, **there is no competition!**

Therefore:

You are not a potential employee selling your services to the highest bidder

Your clients are not employers. The client-coach relationship is a heart-to-heart meeting of equals. You deliver a service they need and the payment reflects the value of that service.

They are not paying you for your time. They are paying for the value of the transformation you facilitate in their lives.

If the change you bring about could be delivered by a hundred, a thousand or even a million other people, then the value is not very high.

If the change you bring is unique to you or is delivered in your own unique manner, the value is very high indeed!

However, since old habits die hard, many coaches are still clinging to the old 'getting the best jobs' strategy and applying it to construct an image of themselves, based on what their Ego believes to be their greatest value.

That value could be built from the feedback they receive whenever they tell someone what they do for a living.

If they have been accustomed to receiving highly favourable feedback when they tell others their job title, that 'Wow, I'm impressed' response may be hard to let go of!

Can you see how tempting it can be to craft a coaching message based on what would impress other people?

Do you see how easy it is to let our beliefs about job titles and prestige influence our authentic message? That's why I said that it can take courage to let go of an impressive job title

In fact, if you ask yourself "Who am I?", what comes to mind?

Is it a job title?

When you tell yourself, or other people, "I'm a Coach" does it feel authentic?

You see: a job title doesn't really cut it, does it?

But we have learned to hide behind the job title. We have become so accustomed to judging ourselves and others according to their job title, that it has become a measure of our worth – and we confuse it with our identity!

You might have spent 30 years telling people at dinner parties 'I'm a Business Consultant' or 'I'm a Nuclear Physicist' and enjoying the feedback from others. You expect the judgement of others to be favourable – they will love you because they think you must be 'smart, educated, high-earning, etc.'

Can you see how that has come from the false beliefs you picked up in the Industrial Era?

**False Belief 1**: Some job titles are more important than others

**False Belief 2**: My value to the World depends on my qualifications and experience

**False Belief 3**: More 'important' job titles are worth more money and will impress others

**False Belief 4**: My authentic self won't be worth as much as these impressive job titles

**False Belief 5**: My purpose is not valuable

**False Belief 6**: Better if I just resist getting clear on who I am and the unique message I deliver. I'll choose something more 'marketable'.

Ultimately, we boast about our status because we want to be seen as *successful*. If you have a Porsche parked in the drive, a second home in Monte Carlo and the freedom to travel and do what you want, do you think anyone cares what your job title is?!

For many coaches, there is a deep-seated fear that giving up that false construct of an impressive job title will lower their status and earning power – to the extent that they would choose to have higher **perceived** social standing than actually be paid well for doing something they love!

I include myself in that number! I established a thriving online marketing business, working with corporate clientele and creating real profit growth for them. I had an impressive job title – I was CEO of an SEO Marketing Company. I saw first-hand the difference between telling people "I'm a CEO" over telling people "I'm a Coach"!!

So, just as I did, people think: "How can I design a coaching title that sounds as impressive as my previous work experience?"

They also want to be seen as successful, so there's a lot of 'fake it 'til you make it' in coaches just starting out.

I see so many coaches trying to create a job title that they *believe* will impress clients and, as a result, building an image of what they *think* other people will buy into, rather than trusting that their authentic self already **IS** something much better, more enjoyable, much more powerful – and much more profitable!

Let me reveal a little secret: your clients don't care what your job title is. They care about *what you can do for them!*

Trust me, what you can do for them – the real results that change their lives – the work that comes from the unique gift that you bring – will be much more impressive and much more rewarding (spiritually and financially) than any job title your mind can devise from your 20$^{th}$ Century limiting beliefs.

As tempting as it may be to copy what is working for other people, you will never make good money by offering the same as everyone else or delivering it the same way.

The strategy of picking a broad area in which you can be of service to a wide range of people not only dilutes the strength of your message, it lets you disappear into a huge, anonymous sea of people doing the same thing.

In that situation, people are unable to see what sets you apart, your unique message. Why should they choose you? What makes you special?

Your ability to coach anything to anyone should not be confused with your *duty* to discover your niche – to get clear on what you should be delivering and to whom.

As we discussed in the previous chapter, the 20$^{th}$ Century approach of depending on someone else to give you a job, led to the tendency to become a Jack-of-all-Trades (i.e. all things to all men).

You were encouraged to spread the net of qualifications and expertise as wide as possible in order to appeal to as many potential employers as possible when your employment opportunities were restricted by geographical area. That strategy no longer applies; it came to an end around the beginning of the century, when the Internet turned the world of work on its head.

Love it or loathe it, the Internet cannot be un-invented. It is here to stay and there is no going back.

As a heart-centred coach, it's time to embrace it and to see it for what it actually is: a remarkable tool that facilitates your connection to that unique group of people who are waiting for the solution you deliver – wherever they are in the World.

# THE JOY OF CONNECTION

*"All money is a matter of belief."*

*Adam Smith*

# THE JOY OF CONNECTION

# CHAPTER 6

## MONEY AND YOUR MESSAGE

Money (or the lack of it!) is a big issue for many coaches and potential coaches.

Some coaches have been so damaged by the value judgements of their self-worth in the industrial era, that they can't bring themselves to charge enough for their services.

Often this arises from having an unclear message. If the coach can't see the value in what they offer, how can they expect a potential client to see it.

Another issue lies in their beliefs surrounding charging money for their calling. After all, it's just helping people, isn't it?

Yes, it is —and the same could be said for a doctor or a lawyer, and many other callings. Would you expect a doctor or a lawyer to work for free? Of course, not.

This requires some explanation, since many coaches, particularly healers and therapists believe that their natural gift is just a duty to deliver and tainting it with the exchange of money seems too commercial or selfish.

There is actually quite a lot of Ego in those beliefs; the idea that somehow our calling is 'above' money. That implies a belief that money itself is somehow wrong or corrupt or not spiritual.

I often meet coaches who say things like "Oh, I'm not in it for the money. I just want to share my gift with the World.", thereby attempting to detach themselves from other people's judgements around money.

Are you refusing to accept the true value of your gift because of other people's false beliefs around money?

Often the coach's reluctance to charge what they are worth stems from their inability to express **exactly** what they do.

They then blame this disconnect between 'what they want to charge' and 'what they think other people are willing to pay' on the potential client, rather than accepting the responsibility for not having taken the time to do the work to get clear on their message and their solution.

How can a potential client see the **value** in what you offer, and whether it applies to them, unless **you can describe that clearly**?

If you are a coach who finds it easy to enlist clients for free coaching, ask yourself "Do my clients value the free coaching I give them?"

Ask yourself whether you value things that are offered free. If you download two training courses offered online, when one is free and one costs $990, which course do you complete? The one with the higher value attached, of course.

So, which course gets results?

It doesn't matter if the free course is a hundred times better than the course with a price tag, you are more likely to get results from the paid course, **because you are more likely to do the work!**

Your clients' results depend on their **commitment** to your coaching.

Remember, too, that your value lies in the **results you obtain for your clients**, which is *not* the same as the number of hours you take to get those results.

If a client has spent two years consulting a psychiatrist about their panic attacks, they might be spending $500 a month and they are still not free of the problem.

If your healing practice gets real results in 2 or 3 sessions, what is the value in that? The client has paid $12,000 to a psychiatrist and still needs more consultations. Should you charge less because you 'only' gave the client 2 hours of your time?

Many coaches are failing their potential clients who are waiting for their services. They are in resistance to charging what their services are worth, or they are offering their services free of charge, thereby failing to show the value of what they deliver.

Does that show respect to the gift with which you have been entrusted?

Are you guilty of devaluing your own purpose?!

Money is neither 'dirty' nor 'good' nor 'bad'. These are all value judgements that we have acquired about money, but are they 'true', and, more importantly, do they serve us or our clients?

**Money is only a physical representation of an exchange of value.**

Every single one of us has the ability to create value. It follows that every single one of us has the ability to create money.

Unfortunately, if you believe that your value only lies in your time, **you** are seriously restricting your ability to make money. Notice, that **you** are doing this – not your clients, nor market forces.

Your clients are waiting for your unique solution.

How many clients will you be able to serve if you give away your services and take on a part-time job to support your calling?

Will you serve more of your clients by charging less or more for your valuable services?

# THE JOY OF CONNECTION

*"The sole purpose of business is service. The sole purpose of advertising is explaining the service which your business renders."*

*Leo Burnett*

# THE JOY OF CONNECTION

# CHAPTER 7

## MARKETING IS NOT A DIRTY WORD,

## IT'S YOUR DUTY!

If you don't reach out to the clients who are waiting for your services, how will they know about you? How will they get the help they need?

Promoting your coaching business is not an optional extra or an inconvenient chore. It is your duty and your obligation to connect with the people you have come to serve.

I hear many coaches complain that their potential

clients don't 'get' them or don't understand why the price for the coaching is so high.

This is not the fault of our clients. It is **our** responsibility to identify the group of people who need our solution, to make contact with them and to explain exactly what we do. That means we have to advertise our businesses – and that requires financial investment and also time. Moreover, it requires us to be able to express clearly what we offer and to whom.

That doesn't mean writing a corporate business slogan to impress our peers. It means taking the time to hone our unique message and define the results we deliver in language which our clients resonate with. We must also be able to describe the niche we serve, using the descriptors they would use for themselves. We must be able to describe their pain in the words they use,  so that they recognise us and know who we are.

Imagine you had just lost a dear friend to a rare skin disease and then discovered that the only consultant in the World with the cure for that disease lived in your town – but you had never heard of him. How would you feel? Angry with yourself for not knocking on every single door in the town – or seriously let down by his failure to advertise his business well enough to the people who needed his unique skills?

The message is clear: don't allow money - or lack of it - to become a barrier to getting your solution to the people who urgently need it.

Stop seeing your coaching practice as 'going to **get** clients' – believing that you are asking, or even begging, people to pay for your time.

It has been said that life is like a buffet – a banquet of many different plates. We each provide a different dish, and each of us is waiting for a particular dish. If you don't provide your unique dish, someone else goes hungry.

Your unique offering is needed for the banquet. It's your duty to understand what you bring and the unique way you deliver it in terms of 'going to **serve** clients'.

# THE JOY OF CONNECTION

*"It's not hard to make decisions once you know what your values are."*

*Roy E. Disney*

# THE JOY OF CONNECTION

# CHAPTER 8

## BELIEFS AND VALUES:

## UNDERSTANDING THE DIFFERENCE

Often we make a sweeping statement about 'my beliefs and values' with the implication that 'beliefs' are the same thing as 'values'. This is not the case and it is important to understand the difference at the outset.

Our values are intrinsic to who we are, but our beliefs are constructed by the mind, based on our experiences of the World around us.

Our values are held in the heart, we don't need to 'do' anything to construct them; they are inherent. These values, and their hierarchy, may alter at different times in our lives, as our circumstances and priorities change, but they are fundamental to who we are and they drive our behaviour.

The heart does not use language to communicate. It uses feelings. Our values cannot be created or altered by the processes of logical thought.

Any attempt to override your core values by means of reasoned argument of the mind will be met with **resistance**.

Consider the 'heart's desire' *versus* the 'mind's belief' disconnect when you attempt to lose weight or give up smoking. The mind may be convinced of the argument for eating healthily or for avoiding a habit that is damaging your health, but if the heart desires a piece of cake or a cigarette, the battle is on!

Notice how that feeling of hunger is translated into ideas such as: "one little piece of cake won't make any difference" or the nicotine craving reminds you that "there are lots of people who smoke and live to be 100 – you have to die of something!"

## The Dangers of Attempting to Impose a Belief that is Inconsistent with Your Values

If our beliefs and values match up, then we are authentic, true to ourselves and at peace.

However, the problem arises when there is a conflict between our beliefs and values. Then we are inconsistent and sabotaged by a heart – mind disconnect, where the mind attempts to implement a decision which is not congruent with the heart's desire. You will never feel at peace while the heart and mind are pulling in opposing directions.

We are not born with our beliefs, but we construct them based on our observations of what happens when we interact with the external world. When an event occurs, we make a judgement about that event and decide that it is 'good' or 'bad', depending on the meaning we assign to it.

Beliefs are neither true nor false, but simply personal judgements which we take on because they serve us, or have served us, for some reason.

Since everyone's experience of the World is different, it is obvious that we all construct our own personalized belief system based on our experiences, and then we make a judgement about a new event by filtering it through the belief system we have set up.

We know that one person's experience of the same event may vary greatly from another's, simply because they are interpreting it through their own personal belief system.

For example, a heavy snowfall may be an exciting prospect for a child who would welcome the opportunity to stay home from school and build a snowman. That same snowfall would be less than welcome to an elderly person who is sensitive to cold and nervous about falling on icy pavements.

The statement 'a heavy snowfall is bad' is neither 'true' nor 'false', but will be true or false for **them** depending on their beliefs about the snowfall.

We take on a belief because it has served us in some way. However, the mind cannot be relied upon to make accurate judgements about situations based on our limited experience, especially if the event happened when we were too young to comprehend the event properly and didn't have the resources to adequately process the meaning at that time.

For example, if, as an adult, you are bitten by a dog, you probably have enough experience of domestic animals to know that most dogs behave well and you just happened to be in the wrong place at the wrong time. However, if you had been bitten by that dog when you were 3 years old, not only would the pain and shock be disproportionately greater to your little body, this event might form your only – and last - experience of dogs.

Even though you lacked insufficient contextual information on which to make a rational judgement, you were likely to form a powerful belief that 'dogs are dangerous'.

At the time, your fear of dogs served you – you avoided coming into contact with dogs and you didn't get hurt!

If, as a child, you developed a belief that dogs were dangerous, in order to protect you from getting hurt, does that same belief serve you later in life? For example, if you find yourself living on a street with several dogs in the vicinity? How does your belief serve you? Would your life be easier if you didn't have to spend so much time worrying about walking down the street, or arriving at the home of your prospective parents-in-law to be greeted by a barking St Bernard?

Many people have developed an irrational lifetime fear of something based on an isolated incident that happened when they were young.

If you were bitten by a dog in infancy, it is easy to identify where your negative beliefs about dogs were formed and why you acquired the fear of dogs to protect you.

Other beliefs may be less easy to identify, but it is still important to look at **why** you acquired a belief and **how** that belief served you. The next step is to ask honestly whether the belief *still* serves you. Notice: that doesn't mean deciding whether the belief is 'true' or not, but whether it gets you where you want to go or sabotages your progress.

We looked at the example of how our beliefs around employment and money may have served us in the world of work prior to the arrival of the Internet.

Not only do they no longer serve us in our calling as coaches, these obsolete, but deeply-ingrained, beliefs are actively sabotaging the work of many coaches right now.

For most people, it is easier to identify beliefs than values.

For that reason, I have presented a list of common values, at the end of this chapter.

This is not intended as an exhaustive list – there are many more – and there is no 'normal'. There is no judgement around this. Your values are you, they are neither good nor bad, they just are.

You may resonate with the whole list or just one or two, and, of course, you will probably have others that don't appear here. Your values may change at different stages in your life, or you may have basically the same values, but the hierarchy will change.

For example you may have values such as freedom and family.

When you are younger, freedom may be more important than family, but when you have small children to look after, family may take precedence over freedom.

I recommend you start by choosing 6 to 10 values that apply to you, and start working with them.

A powerful way to know whether something is a value is to imagine how you would feel if it were taken away from you.

Notice whether you select some values because you **believe** you should have them! That is not authentic! Be wary of adopting other peoples' values!

Remember how we chose a job title or a coaching niche based on what we **believed** other people expected of us? Danger! If your mind constructs your message, your heart is going to give you some serious grief!!

## *A LIST OF VALUES*

| Accomplishment | Enlightenment | Inspiring | Relaxation |
|---|---|---|---|
| Affirmation | Excellence | Integrity | Respect |
| Ambition | Experiencing | Joy | Risk |
| Authenticity | Expression | Loyalty | Security |
| Aesthetic | Fraternity | Love | Self-esteem |
| Being | Faithfulness | Money | Sensitivity |
| Cautious | Family | Marriage | Service |
| Collaboration | Forgiveness | Mentoring | Silence |
| Communication | Freedom | Nurturing | Solitude |
| Community | Frugality | Order | Spirituality |
| Compassion | Fulfilment | Patience | Stability |
| Competition | Fun | Peace | Security |
| Consistency | Gentleness | Perfection | Success |
| Creativity | Genuineness | Performance | Temperance |
| Determination | Growth | Persistence | Tolerance |
| Diligence | Honesty | Power | Tranquility |
| Efficiency | Humility | Productivity | Trust |
| Effectiveness | Humour | Purity | Truth |

# THE JOY OF CONNECTION

| Elegance | Honour | Quality | Winning |
|---|---|---|---|
| Encouragement | Independence | Recognition | |

*"Values are like fingerprints. Nobody's are the same, but you leave them all over everything you do."*

*Elvis Presley*

# THE JOY OF CONNECTION

# CHAPTER 9

# YOUR MESSAGE: THE PROCESS

We have looked at how the training programmes will work once you are clear on your niche. The programmes show you **how** to set up your practice – they are the practical application and are effective. They show you how to build the vehicle that will deliver your message.

Your purpose – your message - is the fuel on which the vehicle runs.

With the right message – that is unique to you – the vehicle will perform well, even if it's a bit rusty or the doors are missing. However, even the best vehicle in the World will not run far on the wrong fuel.

The marketing, the website, the Social Media Posts, the advertising – these are the vehicle, THE HOW.

They are Step 2, and will work effectively when you are clear on Step 1: THE WHAT: your unique message and the solution you bring.

However, so many coaches are attempting to build the vehicle without knowing what fuel it will run on!

That natural inclination to work out the 'how you will do it' before you get clear on 'what you will do' is part of our default human programming.

As you know, the brain is made up of the conscious and the subconscious.

The subconscious takes care of the basic functions of the body, such as breathing and pumping the blood through our veins. We couldn't possibly function if the conscious mind had to remember to breathe!

The subconscious is hard-wired to keep you safe – and to **avoid change at all costs!** It will resist any attempt of the conscious mind to override the programming – like when you try to hold your breath underwater for more than a minute!

When trying to work out something in the conscious mind – the 'What?' – the subconscious mind will always be shouting 'How?' In the background.

So we end up trying to solve two questions – 'What?' and 'How?' simultaneously! Unless you are aware of what is happening between the conscious and subconscious here, the subconscious usually wins – otherwise you might have drowned in that underwater breath-holding competition!

The subconscious mind is happy for you to go off solving the 'How' without getting clear on the 'Why', and, as long as you are occupied with that, it knows you are unlikely to bring about the change it is resisting. It has succeeded in keeping you 'safe'!

Add to that the fact that the mind doesn't actually hold the answers, and you can understand why so many coaches are struggling with this!

Now, the subconscious mind might go along with the conscious mind's idea to improve your situation by leveraging your natural gifts to make more money – and allow you to create the **illusion** that you are making progress. However, as soon as it detects change, it's going to flag up as many danger signals as it can muster to make sure you don't go ahead with altering the status quo!

The **pointless discussion** with yourself goes a bit like this:

Right, I'm going to write a list of the skills and experience I can monetize.

So far so good. The subconscious is quite happy to let your mind wander all over the place – and of course, remind you that you haven't called your sister this week, or that the dog needs to go for a walk or wonder what's for dinner; subtle distractions to scatter your focus so that you appear to be going through the motions of initiating change, but give up without reaching any decisions.

If, however, you do hit upon any ideas, these will immediately be countered with the subconscious best reasons why they won't work.

So now you find yourself struggling with two tasks simultaneously – finding ideas and responding to the subconscious excuses why the ideas won't work.

Result: maybe 10 minutes thought, followed by 5 minutes of why it won't work. Give up – and go to walk the dog.

When we are asked if we gave any thought to what we will do, we can honestly say that we did – but we couldn't think of anything.

Nothing has changed – another win to the subconscious mind!

In order to get past the subconscious mind, you have to temporarily silence it in order to focus on getting clear on the 'Why' first.

However, you are naturally disposed towards solving the 'How' first! So when a training programme comes along with some great software for setting up your website, or a step-by-step guide to running a coaching practice, it's your natural inclination to go along with that. The subconscious is happy! It knows you have a method to do this!! However, even though you know you are called to coaching and you know HOW to do it, you still haven't addressed the 'WHAT' question! The mind is on board, but the heart is furiously transmitting doubt signals to get your attention.

Remember we said that the programmes will work if you are working from your purpose. If you have known your purpose all your life, and can articulate it clearly, you will just apply the training and *whoosh*.

For those who have found their purpose, it's difficult to show the way to those who haven't.

That's where the problems start. Even really successful coaches who have an unlimited supply of hungry clients have difficulty explaining why some coaches are not succeeding with the same training as the coaches who are. They teach that the successful coaches are succeeding *because* they are applying the method.

However, the correct explanation is that the successful coaches are the ones who are clear on their niche first **and** are then applying the method.

The coaching gurus are not trying to mislead you; they just don't understand **why** it is working for them. If they don't know, how can they relay that information to you?

Yes, it is true that **'the method will work for any niche'.** That does **not** mean **'any niche will work for you'!!!**

Please read that sentence until you get it because **this is the missing piece of the puzzle!!**

THE JOY OF CONNECTION

*"Advertising is the ability to sense, interpret...to put the very heart throbs of a business into type, paper and ink."*

*Leo Burnett*

# THE JOY OF CONNECTION

CHAPTER 10

THE THREE ELEMENTS

I mentioned before that words are sometimes inadequate to describe these concepts, and the word 'niche' is not perfect, but it's probably the best we have at the moment and it's understood by most coaches.

However, it is a fairly vague term and is usually a broad description or category rather than a clear definition of what you do.

You may describe yourself as a Business Coach, Life

Coach, Relationship Coach or Healing Coach. Many find this general descriptor – and stop there, usually through fear that being more specific will limit their target client potential. However, as I explained earlier, this is a false belief, a relic of the 'getting a job' strategy and it will seriously hamper your attempts to connect with your clients.

These descriptions can give us a rough idea of the general field you work in, finding your niche is just the beginning – the first element – there is more work to be done.

As a coach, you are called upon to refine your authentic message, from who you are and your core values. You have a duty to be able to describe that message clearly and to express it succinctly in terms of the exact solution you deliver. You must then be able to accurately describe the specific community of people whom you serve.

You are one person. It doesn't make sense for you to have a target audience of 10 million. How could you possibly serve every one of these people?

Some coaches have a message that goes something like:

"I empower Business Managers to Become More

Effective by Optimising their Results."

OK. It conveys a little bit more information than "I'm a Business Coach", and it does, at least, follow the 3 step description of Who, What, How, but what do they actually do?!

-Words like 'business' and 'manager' and 'results' sound impressive and speak to the Ego.

- Who exactly is a 'Business Manager'?

-What does it actually **mean** to 'become more effective', or 'to make more money'?

- How do you help them to 'optimise their results'?

Can you see how hard it is for a potential client to decipher exactly what results you can help them to achieve – and whether, in fact, they actually fit the description of 'Business Manager'?

**In conclusion, the Three Elements of Finding Your Niche are:**

**Element One : Get clear on your message** – the essence of who you are.

This cannot be fabricated from a combination of experience and qualifications, and it cannot be copied from what is working for someone else – it must come from **who you really are**.

**Element Two : Describe the unique way you deliver your message.**

So many coaches get hung up on the old concepts of competition because they believe that other coaches have the same message. Even if other coaches bring a similar message, the **way** in which you deliver your message is unique to you.

Again, **it is up to you to define this clearly.**

**Element Three: Identify your tribe**.

We use the word 'tribe' because there is no word that captures this concept more clearly. These are the specific group of people whom you are called to serve. You must be able to describe them clearly, in words they would use to describe themselves, otherwise, **how will they recognise you?**

Just because your niche cannot be easily pigeon-holed into neat job titles, such as 'teachers' or 'estate agents', that does not absolve you of the responsibility to do the work to define them accurately.

There's work to be done, but, believe me, this will be the most rewarding, satisfying and fruitful work you can do.

You will discover who you really are and free yourself from the doubts regarding your purpose in life.

You will finally **know** who you are and understand the value of the message you have to deliver.

With that clarity, you will automatically receive the **commitment** to serve that precious group of people who are waiting for that solution you bring.

You will break free from the anxiety, the struggle and the doubt, and re-connect to your Joy.

In re-connecting to You, you will discover the Joy of **connection** with the clients who are waiting for you!

# THE NEXT STEP

If you are ready to work with me to finally get clear on your niche, simply drop me a line here to schedule a free Niche Clarity Session:

**hello@thejoyofconnection.com**

or join our community in the Facebook Group:

**TheJoyofConnection**

I am always to delighted to receive your feedback, comments and suggestions. I answer every email personally, so please do get in touch.

Let's share the Joy!

*Enrico*

# THE JOY OF CONNECTION

# ABOUT THE AUTHOR

**Enrico Massani** was born in Paris, to Italian
parents, raised in France, and has lived and worked
in the United Kingdom since 1987.

He has been a coach for nearly 20 years.
His fascination with online marketing
motivated him to discover all he could about
marketing his own coaching business. Ten years
on, he has amassed an encyclopaedic knowledge of
what works online and a systematic approach to
connecting coaches, consultants and change agents
with their ideal clients. His purpose is to help the
messengers to reconnect to their heart and soul,
and to discover their joy in sharing their message.

Enrico is based in Edinburgh, and loves meditation,
hot yoga, socialising and travelling.

# THE JOY OF CONNECTION

18066165R00068

Printed in Poland
by Amazon Fulfillment
Poland Sp. z o.o., Wrocław